A Special Gift

For

Gillian

From

Sherry

Date

25 Dec '96

Message

Shared joy is a double joy
Shared sorrow is half a sorrow

LOVE LEAPS

BARBARA JOHNSON

Revell
A DIVISION OF
Baker Book House Co

LOVE LEAPS
by Barbara Johnson

© 1995 by Barbara Johnson

Originally published under the title *Fresh Elastic for Stretched-Out Moms: A Calendar of Hope, Inspiration, and Fun* by Fleming H. Revell, a division of Baker Book House Company, Grand Rapids, Michigan, 49516, U.S.A.

© 1995: Christian Art, P.O. Box 1599, Vereeniging, South Africa

Designed by: Christian Art

ISBN 0-8007-7149-4

I am absolutely convinced that
life does not happen by chance.
God has a plan; God's plan
is full of His love for us;
and God's plan will succeed!
When we are in the midst of
pain it is hard to believe that,
but I know it's true, and
I've seen it work.

I celebrate me!

I am worth everything.
I am unique.
In the whole world there is
only one me.
There is only one person with
my talents, my experiences
and my gifts.

Today can be a fresh day, a new beginning. This earth suit will be gone one day, traded in for a robe of white – until then I have today to enjoy!

God will bring healing, patience, and comfort when you don't think you can survive another day. Don't grieve over the past; rejoice that God has already planned the future.

MINUTES OF GOLD

Two or three minutes –
two or three hours,
What do they mean in this
life of ours?
But minutes of gold
and hours sublime,
If only we'll use them once
in a while
To make someone happy –
make someone smile.
A minute may dry a little
lad's tears,
An hour sweep aside the
trouble of years.
Minutes of my time, may bring
to an end
Hopelessness somewhere,
and bring me a friend.

Most of us are long past the
time of going to school,
studying, and taking tests.
Most of us are even past
preparing our children
for school and tests.
But no matter what our ages,
we are never too old to learn.

While life isn't always
the way we want it,
no tragedy lasts forever.
Recovery and survival are in
reach. We can walk together,
patiently enduring the sorrow
and depression, as we grow up
from the valley, onto the
mountaintop. Sorrow may flood
you repeatedly, but each time
you will survive, stronger and
happier than before. You will
bounce back quicker and not
stay down so long.

I ran into a classmate the other day, and she had aged so much she didn't even recognize me.

Even when our parental love
seems all spent and wasted,
even when our best intentions
and prayers seem to have
produced children who reject us
and the Lord, God's love
never fails.

It would be great if we could all be spendthrifts and just buy anything in sight. But we can be spendthrifts in love! Love is the one treasure that is multiplied by division. It is the one gift that grows bigger the more you take from it.

No matter what has happened
in the past, that is over.
No matter how much you wish
the past had been different,
you cannot change what has
already happened. Don't mourn
over what is done; rejoice that
there is still a future!

Yesterday is a canceled check,
tomorrow is a promissory note,
but today is cash! Use it wisely.

Nothing is perfect,
nothing will be exactly right,
but we can enjoy and appreciate
what we have, not what we
wish we had. We need to
learn to accept what God
has for us.

This heart of mine is such
a fragile thing.
Like fine porcelain, I could
set it on a shelf,
but I tend to put it rather
in the midst of life.
Thus it has been broken
a million times.
Perhaps the glue with which
God mends it
is stronger than the stuff
of which it is made.

Don't be afraid to share your love. Don't be afraid to give your love to a wayward child. Nothing will happen to you and your love that God isn't ultimately in charge of. He will give you the strength to risk your love, and the glue if your heart breaks and needs mending.

Through the wetness of
your tears, your own sorrow
will begin to glisten.
You can go from the pits,
where it is black, to beige,
and then to rainbows,
which come from tears in
our lives. Your constant habit
of being a joy collector
will be your therapy.

The love of a parent for a child
should be a reflection of the
love God has for each of His
spiritual children. That's a love
that can cause pain.
That's a love that can suffer,
but can't be turned off.
That kind of love is precious.

Prayer is asking for rain and
faith is carrying the umbrella.

Joy is not the absence of suffering, but the presence of God. We all go through pain and sorrow, but the presence of God, like a warm, comforting blanket, can shield us and protect us, and allow the deep inner joy to surface, even in the most devastating circumstances.

Life is a bundle of little things
and the string is always
becoming untied.

Nothing comes into our lives until it first passes through the will of God. He has promised never to leave us or forsake us. Trusting Him is all we can do to carry us through the times when we flounder and see no way ahead of us to go on.

There are two things we can give to our children. One is roots, and the other is wings. Yes, the first is easier to give than the last.

LOVE IS … Slow to suspect
… quick to trust.
Slow to condemn …
quick to justify.
Slow to offend …
quick to defend.
Slow to reprimand …
quick to forbear.
Slow to belittle …
quick to give.
Slow to provoke …
quick to conciliate.
Slow to hinder … quick to help.
Slow to resent …
quick to forgive.

The light of Christ is waiting
just around the corner,
waiting for you to ask for
change and recovery.
Even when we don't think we
see anything positive in our
cicumstances, God's plan
is quietly unfolding
behind the scenes.

You will find Him to be, just as He promised, "a very present help in time of need."

God can heal your heart. God can rescue you from despair and give you something to rejoice about again. It won't happen overnight, but it will happen. All you have to do is be willing to give every piece of your broken heart to God.

There's an old Swedish proverb which says, "Shared joy is a double joy. Shared sorrow is half a sorrow."

God's love is expressed through other people to us. You don't have to be a perfect saint to be able to share love with someone else. You don't even have to be especially mature as a Christian to share God's love. You just have to be willing and open.

Perhaps the best thing about
the future is that it comes
just one day at a time.

Experience is the hardest kind of teacher … it gives you the test first and the lesson afterwards.

Recently I developed a neat idea someone suggested to me: "Life isn't what you want, but it's what you've got, so stick a geranium in your hat and be happy!"

Fertilizer is plant food and faith is soul food. Without fertilizer, your garden cannot flourish, and your spirit cannot grow without faith.

I know God will help you.
I know God will heal you.
I know that there is hope.
I have been there,
I have been restored.

God always keeps His promises. You will get through and you will get back in the flow of life.

We have to give our children to God and then take our hands off. It is like wrapping a package up and putting on a label, and then being able to send it, without our special directions of where to go, but letting God put the address on the label – or on that life.

Give yourself some love homework this month. Assign yourself the task of loving someone you don't really like. I don't mean that you will make yourself her best friend, but determine (make a decision of the will) that you will be obedient to Christ and love her, in spite of her shortcomings. God will bless you for that.

God removes the sting, and
time does allow us to remember
the good, while painful
memories seem to fade away
like water-colored pictures
in the rain.

The value of fun lies in the spirit of it, whether it is climbing windmills, or marching in a parade, or going up on the down escalator. Break out of your little plastic mold and become a real dingy person (not din-gee, but ding-ee), even if people think you are fresh out of a rubber room. Laughing helps. It's like jogging on the inside.

Look at people and marvel
at how each one is a
unique reflection of God's
creative diversity. Look at
a field of flowers and see
flowers, not weeds.

When we have problems in our lives which seem so often to have no reason, and we lack any understanding of them, we have to rely completely on the lighthouse of God's direction for our lives and the rock of Christ's salvation.

What is the bottom line on aging and dieting? The bottom line is that your future is in God's hands, not yours.

Love doesn't have to be profound, or educated, or dazzling. It just has to be there, steady and sure, even in the bad times.

When life gets so heavy for you, and you wonder how you can cope with all the load, learn to put on the garment of joy for the spirit of heaviness – and fun is included in that garment of joy.

Give yourself at least one
success experience today. It
could be doing exercises
you hate or completing
an unpleasant task.

We must always remember that God hates sin and yet is so tender and compassionate toward the sinner.

Do whatever makes you laugh – tasting Christmas on old pine branches, or hibernating with old "I Love Lucy" reruns. Find some way to flatten out your pain.

Hope springs eternal, and
is held by the bedrock of
God's love.

In the midst of your grief, just hang on to the idea that this too will pass, and God will use it for good.

Who can describe hope to anyone? Hope is that light at the end of the tunnel, when all around you is black.

Finding a refuge . . . isn't that what we are all doing? People who hurt as we hurt need a place to cry, a person to care, the security of intimate friends who will share our hurt.

Often we cannot see the
fruits of our work, and so think
our work has been in vain.
In God's service somewhere
all our acts of love bear fruit,
and some heart receives their
blessing and joy.

Keep sending out love messages and planting love seeds in your family.

You are growing, you are changing, you are maturing, you will win, with God's help.

Your child is in God's hands –
let Him take the burden of
your sorrow and build victory
through your hope. This isn't
the end of your life. It's the
beginning of your future.

Happiness and hope are so closely intertwined that it seems as though if we just grab onto that little bit of hope, it pulls us up out of the pit enough to remember that happiness is possible.

Offer yourself to God and ask for a spirit of pardon so your being will be restored. Tears and sorrow come, but each time God will be there to remind you that He cares.

In this process of healing and becoming, which we are all in, let us reach out and help others find that place of comfort, pointing others to the one shelter of God's care, a refuge for a wounded one.

"Finally, brothers, whatever
is true, whatever is noble,
whatever is right, whatever
is pure, whatever is lovely,
whatever is admirable – if
anything is excellent
or praiseworthy – think
about such things."

– Philippians 4:8

If you can put one touch of rosy
sunset into the life of another,
you should feel that you have
worked with God.

There is no way to silence the grief of having to mourn a loved one who has not died.

Nobody is a perfect parent, and there are no trial runs at parenting. We just love our kids and do our best – God doesn't demand anything more.

Have you ever been in the
desert at night and seen the
glistening stars twinkle brightly?
All around us we can find
sparkling jewels from God
scattered in our dark places –
if only we look for them.

There is no oil without
squeezing the olive,
No wine without pressing the
grapes,
No fragrance without
crushing the flowers,
And no joy without sorrow.

Take God's comfort blanket
of love, wrap it snugly around
you, and enjoy the warmth and
protection it offers.

Joy doesn't have to be expensive. You don't have to sell your family jewels (if you have any) to buy joy. Joy is thoughtfulness. Joy is caring. Joy is saying, "Thank you, God," for life.

We cannot let our burdens paralyze our progress.

Call two favorite people
and tell them how much
you love them.

Lord, have mercy and show
Your pardon and love to my
child this day.

Joy from loved ones can be a very simple and very powerful encourager. Recognize the joy those who love you are holding out to you, and think of how you can be a spirit lifter to someone else.

Take a friend to lunch. Talk about all the good things in the world. Or make up with an old friend.

Take a walk through a park, or explore a new area. See how much beauty you can find along the way.

Spoil yourself a little.
Buy something you've
always wanted.

We can choose to gather to our hearts the thorns of disappointment, failure, loneliness, and dismay in our present situation. Or we can gather the flowers of God's grace, boundless love, abiding presence, and unmatched joy. I choose to gather the flowers.

Love always:
Protects – I want to take the
hurt for my child. Instead,
I will protect and love him.
Trusts – I trust, even when
my husband travels a lot and
faces life's temptations.
Hopes – We still share our
dreams for life together.

Make a list of your blessings.
Include everything good that's
ever happened to you.

Whatever you write
On the heart of a
child,
No water
can wash it
away.

– Author unknown

To see anger and bitterness and hardness disappear, to be replaced by a gentle spirit and overflowing love, is exciting!

If you spend a lot of time watching television, decide today you will watch only one good program.

My family and I know we love each other. We know that our love, based in the love of God, has withstood the test and is stronger than ever. No matter what happens, we love each other, no strings attached.

Hope and miracles are almost synonymous. Sometimes our hope seems to invite God to do a miracle in our lives. Sometimes our hope gets a much-needed boost from a miracle sent just for that purpose.

God's Love Letter to You

Dwell in My power and in My love and be free! Be yourself! Don't allow other people to run you. I will guide you, if you let Me. Look to Me for your answers.

When we have hope, we are showing that we trust God to work out the situation. Trust is the only way we're going to make it through and be a part of God's marvelous plan for our child.

When you are low down, with arms drooping down and bent knees, then read Hebrews 12:12: "Wherefore lift up the drooping hands and the feeble knees."

We cannot change the past,
but we can ruin a perfectly good
present by blaming ourselves
for past mistakes.

There is a risk to loving your child: you are vulnerable. You can get hurt. But the reward and the responsibility can give you a maturity, a close love, and a relationship nothing can ever replace.

We have failed in many areas of our lives, but failing doesn't make us failures! We have to learn from our mistakes, and learn how to prevent them in the future.

Lord, as I trust You this moment for my own peace and assurance, I also trust You to care for my child's needs.

Take the risk, let yourself go, love your child. No matter what suffering you go through later, the laughter you experience now will build you strong for those times of testing.

Stop what you are doing long enough to enjoy the sunset, listen to a special song that lifts you up, or pick up the phone and share some special thought with a caring friend.

We know that when we get to the end of the rope, we tie a knot and hang on . . . but do you know what that knot at the end of the rope is called? It is hope. That's the possession of each Christian, because we have a solid basis for hope.

Lord, forgive me my sins and overlook my mistakes. Bring to me your comfort. Relax all of the parts of my mind and emotions that are tense and burdened down.

We must be frank and honest with God on what we have done wrong. Then we must relinquish it to God, give to Him our failures, and reach out and accept God's cleansing forgiveness.